Just Us

For Homicidal Bereavement
By Wanda Henry-Jenkins
Illustrated by Ron Boldt

Just Us, two small words which define the plight and capture the essence of what if feels like to be survivors or murder victims.

**Overcoming and Understanding Homicidal Loss and Grief
Includes Bereavement Impact Statement**

Centering Corporation Resource
Revised 1997
©Copyright 1993
All Rights Reserved

ISBN#1-56123-059-6
SAN#298-1815

Centering Corporation is a small, non-profit bereavement publishing company. Please write or call for more information on all our available resources.

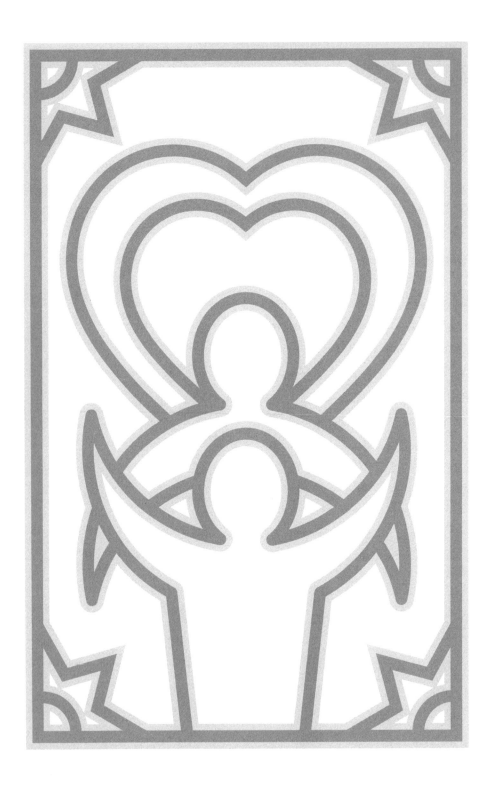

The Journey Begins - Part I

Momma's Homicidal Death

On a cold winter night in February, my 17-year-old sister, Tillie (Aquilla is her real name), walked away from the large picture glass window in the living room of Momma's house. My 11-year-old sister, Gina, was asleep in the front bedroom with Tillie's 2-year-old son, Marc and 1-year-old daughter, Juanita. Nightly, Tillie waited at the window for Momma to come home from work. She glanced at the clock. It was a few minutes before midnight. She watched out the window and noticed that freshly fallen snow had lightly covered the ground. She knew that Momma should be arriving home soon.

Momma, Juanita Sussewell Henry, was working the second shift as a licensed practical nurse at Northwest Memorial Hospital. Normally, she worked the day shift and did not like to work the second shift. However, all day-time nursing personnel had to rotate hours periodically. The hospital was located on Chicago's northside in the North Shore Gold Coast area. Momma's house was an hour away on the city's south side, in the Englewood section. She did not drive, which meant she had to take public transportation. Momma was a very systematic person who followed certain routines. Whenever she worked the second shift, she would wait for a bus at the rear entrance of the hospital. She would ride the bus about a mile to the subway and take the subway to 63rd and Wentworth Streets. There she would hail a taxicab and ride it to her house. She knew that Tillie would be watching out of the window and waiting for her to arrive home. In Chicago, muggings and murder rates were high and rising daily. Momma's routine was designed to assure her safety.

The clock on the living room wall showed it was after midnight. Tillie had just walked away from the window and was heading in the direction of the dining room when she heard a car door slam. Suddenly, the night's serenity was broken by a gunshot. As Tillie rushed back to the window, she heard Momma's desperate voice scream out, *Tillie Tillie, I'm the one who has been shot. Call the police, I'm shot!* Tillie looked out the window and saw Momma coming up the steps shouting. *Call the police, I'm shot.* Tillie opened the door and then ran to the telephone and dialed 911. She told the operator, *My mother has been shot! Send the police to 520 W. 62nd Street.* She ran back to the door to help Momma.

Momma had struggled into the living room. The collar of her beige coat and her white uniform were drenched with blood. There was blood all over her hands as she grabbed the wall to steady her faltering steps. No longer strong enough to hold herself up, Momma slid to the floor and was semi-conscious.

The police arrived within minutes. They tried to get Momma to tell them who had shot her. She gazed at them and tried to speak. Everyone in the room listened intently, but her garbled words were only desperate whispers and incoherent sounds. So no one, not the police nor my sisters understood the final words Momma struggled to utter. Suddenly, she stopped talking and dropped her head. Momma slipped into a coma.

The policemen lifted her onto a cart and into the back of the police van. They knew she was dying. They did not want Tillie to ride with Momma but Tillie persisted. She did not want our mother to lay in the back of a dark van by herself. The police officers reluctantly agreed. Tillie checked Momma's pulse. The rate was so rapid, it could not be counted. Tillie checked Momma's respiration. Her breathing was thready and too shallow to see. She knew Momma was almost dead. When they arrived at the hospital, Momma was taken into the emergency room where they tried for 45 minutes to save her life. Our mother, Juanita Sussewell Henry, age 50, was pronounced Dead On Arrival at 12:30 a.m., February 12, 1972.

"Wanda, I Have Something Terrible to Tell You."

Unlike Momma, I enjoyed working the second shift as a charge nurse in a nursing home because it enabled me to have an active social life. However, on February 12, I went home early. It had been an especially difficult and trying day. I was tired and was in bed by 11:30 p.m. I had been sleeping for a few hours when I heard an insistent knock at my apartment door. I looked at the clock on the table next to my bed. It was 3:00 a.m. I could not imagine who was at my door. I put my robe on and went to the door. *Who is it?* I asked. *It's Tillie,* my sister said.

I knew something was wrong when I saw Tillie and my friend, Dale, standing there. I felt anxious and somewhat fearful. Jokingly, I said, *This better be good.* The expression on Dale's face was sad and apprehensive. It was as if he was not sure what to expect from me. Inside my chest, my heart had begun to beat faster, I knew someone had died. Tillie said, *Wanda, I have something terrible to tell you.* She looked as if she were trying to assess my reaction before telling me. I said, *Who died?* In my head I was trying to determine which one of my family I could live without. I decided none of them. I was not prepared for her response.

Momma is dead.

I screamed, *Oh, no! You must be kidding,* I ran into my bathroom and slammed the door. Once inside and alone, I fell to my knees praying and begging God to let what Tillie said be a lie, a mistake, anything but true. But I knew this was no prank. After fifteen minutes or so, I stopped crying and pleading to God, washed my face, composed myself and came out of the bathroom.

I wanted to know how Momma had died. I needed to understand and make sense out of it. I began to question Tillie. *Did Momma have a heart attack?* I knew she had aortic stenosis (a small or narrow heart artery).
No, said Tillie.
Was it a stroke? It made sense that her blood pressure could have risen and caused a stroke. After all, her grandmother had died of a stroke.
No, Momma was. . .
I anxiously interrupted her. . .*Then what did she die from?* I asked loudly. Nothing, absolutely nothing or no one in the world could have prepared me for Tillie's next words.
Wanda, Momma was shot.
I was wiped out by this news. It was incomprehensible.
You mean Momma was murdered?! I asked. I was confused and bordering on rage.

My mother was dead. Someone had destroyed her life and taken her away from us. It did not make sense. My reaction to my mother's murder was confusion, numbness, smoldering rage, and a need for justice and retribution. I just could not understand how this could happen to my mother, me or my family. The intensity and instability of my emotions were unfamiliar to me. I was 23 and had experienced other losses, death included. Yet, the impact of homicidal loss was different from anything I had ever gone through. It violated everything I believed about human goodness, as well as what I thought about life and death. Murder, or so I thought, happened to bad people, it was a stigma, not related to an honorable death. My mother was a good person and deserved to die with dignity and honor.

I think it is important to tell you how I felt about and faced life and living prior to Momma's murder. In two words I'd say, *protected* and *safe*. As I grew up, my parents provided me with the support I needed to feel secure. No matter what happened, Daddy and Momma were always there for me during a life threatening bout of pneumonia, a serious car accident, an unfair teacher in junior high school, a fight, a broken heart from a canceled wedding, a major surgery and death of a loved one. But facing this type of loss was more than I was prepared to handle. I felt totally ripped apart.

I fully expected that one day I would bury my parents. Included in our upbringing, my parents had prepared my siblings and me for their death. Yet, I had never envisioned or ever thought that either one of them would be a murder victim. After all, we did not associate with those kind of people or do the type of things which can get a person killed. We minded our own business and were a Christian family. I did not realize that truly horrible things could happen to good, decent people.

My Life Was Irrevocably Changed

When I arrived at Momma's house, the first thing I noticed was the blood on the walls and floor. Then I saw the bag with her bloody clothes in it. I never knew why the police had not taken her clothing as evidence. Maybe they sensed that this crime would never be solved. I do not really know. One thing I do know is the sight of her blood on the walls and floor brought immense fear within me. I will never forget what I saw or felt that night. My life was irrevocably changed.

There is never a day that Momma's murder is not with me. In the beginning, her homicide lived within me. My grief was suppressed, and my fears grew. I became less active during the evening hours. I was home by dark unless I had an escort or was with a group of friends. I worked the third shift and took a cab to work. In some way, I imagined that by working all night I was protecting my own life. The more protective I became, the less I left home except out of necessity and the more weight I gained. Within six years after Momma's death, I gained 100 extra pounds. It was as if the layers of fat would scare off a thief or dull the impact of a bullet. Intellectually, I knew better, but emotionally I needed some physical sign of protection or strength.

Faced with Momma's horrible death, I was forced to deal with the severe problems of homicidal loss and grief. None of my family was prepared for loss by homicide. The saddest aspect of her death is that we all felt something; yet none of us shared or discussed this tragedy that changed our lives. We didn't know what to say to each other. Other relatives and friends were grieved and vulnerable. None of us seemed able to comfort and support each other. We tried to treat her death as if it occurred through natural circumstances. My mother had always talked to us about our feelings and thoughts when a family member or friend died. We were free to mourn the loss, grieve together and share our sorrow. But this time was entirely different. Murder had not only taken away our mother, it had also destroyed our ability to mourn and share our grief.

Aborted Grief

Each time we would begin to mourn, the police were there to ask more questions about my mother's lifestyle in order to try to apprehend the person responsible for her death. I felt as if one of us was a suspect. It was extremely aggravating and aborted our grief process. Not only was our grief interrupted, it was stopped completely. If not the police, newspaper reporters called and came to our home to record our anger and sorrow. We had no privacy. It was as if Momma and all her family members had become "celebrities for a day." We were expected to share our loss with the world.

The intrusions on our grief came from many directions and they were overwhelming. I thought that after the funeral it would end and we would be able to regain control of our lives. It did not. It seemed that everyone else was in control of us. The police investigation and news media reports dominated my family's life for weeks and months. Over a period of time, not expressing and sharing our grief alienated us from one another. It was as if when Momma was murdered our family was killed also.

Isolation

I don't know if crime victims assistance was available in Illinois when Momma was killed in 1972. I do know that not I nor any member of my family was ever contacted or given any support in coping with the tremendous aftermath of murder. I turned to my church and found that most pastoral professionals had no sense of how to minister to the bereaved on a long-term, on-going basis. I was told

God wouldn't put any more on me than I could bear. I heard *This too shall pass*. Oh, yes, and another worn-out phrase to comfort me was, *God called Juanita home. . .it was her time to die*. I thought to myself, *These people are crazy*. *Murder is too much for me; her homicide will not just pass over, and are they saying God is a murderer?*

No one was helping us, but everyone wanted something from us. The police wanted information. The news reporters wanted stories. Friends and family members wanted us to tell them over and over again what had happened. The Church wanted us to blindly accept that her murder was the divine will of a loving God. Everyone expected us to pick up our lives after the funeral and return to a normal life. With all the advice we were given, no one told us how we could live or feel joy again.

Just how were we supposed to live after the heart of our family had been so suddenly and violently ripped away? How were we supposed to feel safe and regain our trust in humanity? How were we supposed to resolve her death and our grief as long as her murder remained unsolved? How does a family close an open wound? Neither the church nor the psycho-social community had services to address our unique bereavement needs. Our family was incapable of helping one another. I had no family support, no bereavement and grief intervention, no support from the psychological, religious, or victim's assistance communities. I felt abandoned and isolated.

I am a Survivor

For five years my anger and grief remained suppressed and unresolved. I went on with my life, hiding my grief so that others were comfortable around me. I learned that relatives and friends cannot cope with long-term grief. They don't want to talk about the loss or the deceased after the funeral. Therefore, I did not openly grieve or speak about my mother's homicidal death.

Daily, I grew more fearful and became extremely cautious. I began to develop and establish elaborate schemes to protect my personal welfare. I would not ride on an elevator with a stranger. In fact, I would walk up twenty flights of stairs rather than ride an elevator. I used the excuse that I needed the exercise when questioned about this behavior. I also stopped going out after dark alone, and when out at night I often found myself looking over my shoulder.

After coping with Momma's death so long on my own, I was not happy or secure. My personality had changed. I was distant, argumentative and defensive. When I blew up at my pastor, an older cousin suggested that I see a counselor. I resented her interference and felt she was questioning my mental stability. Intermittently, over the next year, I thought about her recommendation. Furthermore, I was sick and tired of feeling overwhelmingly sad and scared.

So, in the sixth year after Momma's death, I found a psychologist who provided bereavement counseling. I discovered that all of the things which had happened in the aftermath of Momma's murder had aborted and delayed my grief. I knew that I had to face and accept the loss as well as grieve it. The psychologist helped me cope with the bereavement and resolve my grief. Finally, I was free to begin the reorganization of my life and re-enter society healthy and whole.

Understanding Homicide Bereavement

In addition to being a nurse, I had entered the ministry the year my mother was murdered. I had written papers and journal articles on bereavement, grief and homicide. Now, I wanted real answers. I wanted to know why I had responded so differently to Momma's death versus other losses. Was something wrong with me? Did other survivors of homicide victims have similar reactions?

In my last year of college, the seventh year after the murder, I began seeking out other survivors and asking how they felt about the homicidal loss of their loved ones. I asked my family members and friends to share their feelings with me.

I began to provide individual counseling to survivors of murder victims. I began to attend crime victim seminars and started to search for a self-help group of people who had also lost a parent or loved one to murder. In 1986, I learned about a group for family members of murder victims. I attended their meetings. Through it all, I came to understand several things:

1. There was a definite pattern to the bereavement process following homicidal death of a loved one.
2. There was secondary victimization of survivors of murder victims in the aftermath of homicide.
3. There was a need for a grief center for grieving families.

9

4. There was a need to reduce and\or eliminate the stigma and social isolation of survivors of murder victims.

5. Finally, there was a need for survivors to develop a means to commemorate and celebrate their deceased loved one's life.

I, along with others, designed and implemented a Grief Facilitator Training Institute to teach bereaved survivors of murder victims how to develop support groups and help others.

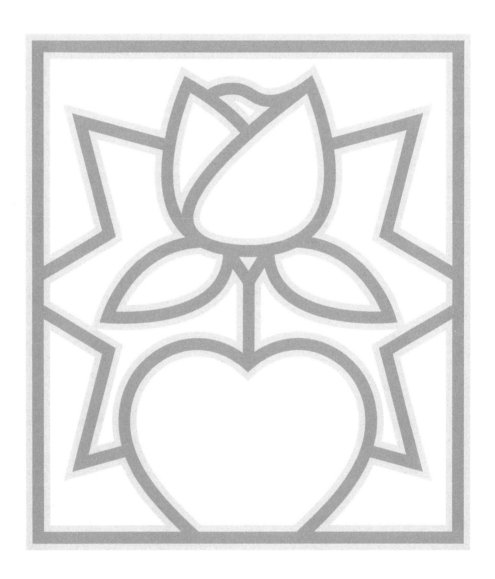

Homicide Hurts! Definitions and Classifications
The Murder of James

On July 17, at 1:30 a.m., Belinda checked on her children. She noted that all of them including her oldest son, 19-year-old James, were sleeping in their beds. Belinda went to bed and slept soundly. At some time during the night, no one knows exactly when, James got up and went to a friend's house. While visiting the friend, James got sleepy, lay down on a cot in the living room and drifted off to sleep.

James was at a different kind of home. Forty-eight hours before going to that house, his mother and step-father warned him to stay away from it. *James, you need to keep away from that house. We understand it's a drug house. And if you keep hanging around with those kinds of people, someone's going to shoot your head off,* his parents told him.

I can run fast, James told his parents.

His mother reminded him, *You can't outrun a bullet.*

James felt his mother and stepfather were overly concerned. To his own detriment and death, James silently crept out of his home.

Shortly before 5:30 a.m., James was abruptly awakened from his sleep to the sounds of gunshots in the room. He saw two male friends lying wounded on the floor. He jumped up and ran for the basement. As he started down the stairwell, the assailant ran behind him and shot him in the back of the head. *Oh!* was the last word a man hiding in the basement heard James utter as his body fell down the steps. Although he was dead when he hit the floor, the murderer ran down the stairs and fired more shots into James' body, mutilating his chest and arm.

Belinda's Story

Belinda woke up that Sunday morning to a nightmare. A relative had been in a neighborhood store and heard that a young man fitting James' description had been shot. She and her husband, Jimmy, hurried to tell Belinda. Belinda's greatest fear had become a reality. She and her husband went to the hospital. Nurses told them their son was in surgery. After Belinda and Jimmy sat in the waiting room for more than six hours, she asked if her husband could just see the child who was in surgery. The doctor permitted Jimmy to view the young man on the operating table. It was not James.

Belinda said, *I felt my child was dead. I just couldn't feel his presence in the hospital.* Finally, the doctor learned that James' body had been taken to the morgue. Belinda's mind reeled. *This can't be happening to me. I have always been able to prevent such tragedies. It's all a mistake.* But it was true. Her second child and first son was a murder victim.

At the morgue, Belinda screamed and cried. She could only see the diamond earring in James' ear. His body was a mess.

Belinda was an executive secretary for a major public transportation line. After her son's funeral, she went back to her job. However, after three months she began to notice specific changes in her behavior and work habits. Belinda realized she was no longer able to remember or complete simple assignments. Her supervisor suggested she take advantage of the company's health plan and seek counseling. Belinda was also concerned because she had not been able to manage household duties or express affection for her husband and children. *I was a basket case. I couldn't cook, clean or care about anything. The way my child died was constantly on my mind.*

Belinda admits she was angry at her son because James should have been in bed sleeping.

She began to receive psychological and bereavement therapy. For six months she was unable to address her anger because of frustration. The accused murderer of her son had escaped to another state. It took law enforcement six months to trace him and extradite him back to the county where he committed the crime. At this point, Belinda was able to relax and start to address her emotional needs. When she attended the pre-trial hearing, her anger accelerated. She had hoped secretly that the murderer would have some remorse. He didn't. Once again, Belinda was devastated. She could not understand how anyone could be so vicious and uncaring. *He was arrogant and just did not care about what he had done to my James. I don't want him to go to the electric chair. That's too easy. I want him to live every day with what he has done.*

By the time Belinda went to the murder trial, 18 months had gone by. Throughout the trial, she stared at the murderer and watched his smugness. His arrogance was too much for her to stomach. Although she did not believe in capital punishment, his attitude changed her mind. She wanted him, the man who had killed her son and another young woman, to be given the maximum penalty,

12

death. He was convicted and received the death penalty. Belinda was relieved. *I'm glad it's all over. Now I feel my son is at peace.* But she still wondered how anyone could be so inhuman and cruel.

Statistics

Homicide hurts! Understanding the human savagery is difficult and virtually impossible. Frankly, I will never pretend to comprehend murder. Neither will Belinda or any other survivor. This is why I believe it is important to know what the facts and myths are surrounding murder.

You are not alone. Murder is at epidemic proportions in the United States. While numbers vary, it is agreed that there are tens of thousands of killings in our country annually.

Definitions and Classifications

So, what **is** murder? Experts say that homicide and murder are terms that have the same meaning. Murder occurs when one human being deliberately, recklessly or accidentally takes the life of another.

Three labels describe homicide: criminal, excusable and justifiable. The majority of people murdered each year are victims of criminal homicide. Criminal homicide happens when a person deliberately or recklessly causes the death of another. For survivors, this is the most senseless and preventable of the three major types. It is known in most states as first degree murder and usually carries the highest penalty of life imprisonment or death. Many of you may want your loved one's murderer to be charged with first degree. When the charges are less, many feel the victim's life is somehow devalued.

Another classification in criminal homicide is second degree murder. This occurs when the homicide is intentional but without premeditation. Penalties vary from state to state, but usually people are sentenced to 10 years to life imprisonment.

Manslaughter involves killing during an unlawful act such as a mugging, a fight, a quarrel or a holdup. It is classified as an unintentional act. A sentence of from 1 to 20 years is common.

Excusable and justifiable homicide occurs when a person kills someone while trying to save another person's life or in self-defense.

Myths and Stereotypes

There are several myths associated with murder. They are detrimental for three reasons:

1. *Stereotypes* - which say that only certain people are murder victims - blacks, gang members, criminals, ghetto dwellers and bad people. I once thought murder only happened to those kinds of people.

2. *Stigma* - there is a secondary victimization where society causes additional pain and suffering by attributing partial blame for the death to the victim and/or the survivors - to you and me.

3. *Social Support* -Myths let people ignore the emotional and social support needs of the survivors of murder victims. This can force us to deny our grief and suppress our emotional pain in order to remain a part of our social environment.

One common myth holds that homicide is a racial crime. It is not. In fact, murder is an intra-racial crime and usually occurs within a specific ethnic culture: 94% of blacks kill blacks; 88% of whites kill whites. Out of thirty cases of homicidally bereaved clients I counseled in one year, not one murder was result of a racial incident.

Society also holds to the erroneous belief that strangers kill each other and people don't know their murderers. In the majority of homicides, the murderer and victim are known to each other. Except for one, all of my clients' deceased loved ones knew and were well-acquainted with their murderers. Many victims died at the hands of a family member, a friend, a neighbor, a business associate or fellow drug dealer.

Another belief is that only certain kinds of people kill. This myth is rooted in classism, sexism and racism. As we know from newspapers, books and television, murderers come from all generations and all cultural, economic, educational, and racial backgrounds. For some killers, homicide was the final outcome of a criminal background. For others, it was the direct result of a violent argument. For some it was the result of a reckless accident. Then for a few, murder was the result of a total mental breakdown. In essence, all types of people commit murder.

It is easier for society and survivors to accept murder if the blame can be placed on society's mental and social misfits. But, it is important to know the facts. This enables us to deal realistically with homicidal loss, not develop stereotypes and hopefully reduce the second victimization of the survivors.

Secondary Victimization

For survivors, there is no escape from the searing pain and sense of victimization following murder. To this victimization is added a second one caused by intrusions immediately after the death. This period is fraught with professional and social responsibilities. Understanding the obligations and duties of those professionals with whom you come in contact after your loved one's murder may enpower you to understand and reconcile what has happened to you and your family, develop a new respect for the procedures that professionals have to carry out and allow you and your family to grieve the loss.

The Police

One of the first professionals you probably met were the police. For many of you, this was your first contact with law enforcement. You were not prepared for the amount of time it took for the police to thoroughly investigate. The first officers at a crime scene usually record the events as reported to them. They do not carry out the investigation. A homicide detective is assigned to every murder case. This person is a trained specialist in murder investigation. The primary role of the homicide detective is to solve the murder, therefore the investigation period may be lengthy, especially in the case of unsolved murders.

My mother's murder was unsolved. There were no witnesses. The ongoing presence of the police officers was a major stress factor for us. It seemed that the homicide detectives visited my house every two hours for the first two days. My family and I told the story over and over again for what seemed like a thousand times. When the homicide detectives showed up the night of the funeral, I had it. I told them, *You have not found out who killed my mother in seven days. So, leave us alone so we can go to the funeral in peace.* There were times when it felt like we were suspects.

You, too, may have been upset about the length of time it took for the police to complete their investigation. Maybe you thought the police were insensitive. Homicide detectives do care about your loss. However, in order to serve the public they must be free to complete their work. Don't worry about how you acted during the investigation. An experienced investigator knew you were suffering. Although they may have felt empathy for your situation, the homicide detectives could not become personally involved with you.

It is perfectly alright and very wise to establish a working relationship with the police. You may periodically check on the progress of the case. Also, in a case where the suspect has avoided arrest, you may call the police to find out if an arrest has taken place. In both of these situations, a homicide detective will usually courteously answer your questions. Some detectives will call you when the case is solved or the suspect is arrested.

Primarily, the homicide investigator's responsibilities are to gather, examine and assess all information and evidence. Then they are to apprehend, arrest, and imprison the murder suspect. After this, the investigators turn all information over to the district attorney's office. Detectives testify at all hearings and court trials.

The man who murdered Belinda's son, James, escaped to another state. For six months the police investigated every lead until they apprehended and arrested him. During the period between the murder and the arrest, Belinda was able to establish a workable relationship with the homicide investigating officer. She was notified when the murderer was caught and would be brought back.

The News Media

Another group of professionals who may contribute to secondary victimization are reporters. They investigate the crime to report the news verbally or in print. For many, media behavior is traumatizing. Many of them are very good in their craft, whereas others will do anything to get the story. I remember the one newspaper reporter who asked if my siblings and I would stand on the porch for a picture. Since that was not the way I wanted my family portrayed, I said, *No.* Maybe you felt used by the news media. Its not an uncommon feeling for average citizens. No one knew who Juanita Sussewell Henry or James Bagwell were before their murders. The notoriety of their deaths catapulted them and us into the glaring spotlight of action news reports. My firmness kept me from becoming victimized by the press. However, I remember my obsession with watching every news report during the first week of Momma's murder. It was as if hearing about her made her life worthwhile.

Ongoing Media reports can be an additional trauma. Belinda said, *I hated seeing my son's body bag paraded across the television screen every time they mentioned his murderer's case.* Eventually, her mixed feelings toward the media were resolved. A newspaper reporter printed Belinda's story about who James was to her.

Depending on the visibility of a murder, the news media will be involved to some degree. You are not powerless. If you have not gone to trial, think about it now and decide how much you want to say to the press. You can determine how you will be treated and portrayed. You can:

choose one family member or friend to be press spokesperson
prepare a written statement and read it,
set a limit on the number of questions you will answer,
set a time limit on the press conference.

You do not have to answer any questions that make you uncomfortable. If you have a favorite local news anchor, you may want to call her and tell her you want to talk to her alone. But remember, above all, be honest. It is better for you to share sensitive information than to have it discovered by an investigative reporter. An experienced and empathetic reporter will report your story accurately and respectfully.

The Autopsy

Aside from the police investigation and news media, another process must take place. An autopsy must be done in every murder case, whether the victim is discovered dead at the scene or dies later in a hospital. The body of the victim is considered evidence and must be examined. An autopsy is a physical examination of the body after death. It involves a careful medical exam of internal organs and the external body to determine the exact cause of and factors which contributed to the death.

A medical doctor performs the autopsy. In rural areas this may be a general practitioner or family doctor. In large cities there is usually a medical doctor who specializes in pathology. The doctor is sometimes called a coroner or a medical examiner. As an expert, the coroner may be a witness for the prosecution or defense. The autopsy findings may help convict or acquit. In some cases, the medical examiner's findings may prevent an unnecessary trial.

Funeral and burial plans may be delayed by the autopsy depending on the medical examiner's facility, available staff and number of autopsies performed daily. Once it has been completed, family members will be notified. In most cases, two people are required to identify the body and sign a verification of identification form. Years ago, when my mother was murdered, the body was brought right up to you. Today, many modern facilities show the body through a television screen. For some families this is more than enough. Others want and need to touch their loved one. My father identified my mother's body. I did not want to see her until the viewing on the night before the funeral. Several survivors I have interviewed would have preferred to actually see and touch their loved one's body.

After the victim is identified, the medical examiner's office will contact the funeral director of the family's choice to pick up the body. Some families may choose to call the funeral director themselves. Whatever is done, see that it meets your family's needs as well as the needs of the medical examiner's department.

The medical examiner's office held a coroner's inquest to verify the cause of death in my mother's case. It was set up like a small courtroom. My family, the medical examiner, the homicide detectives and several men on the coroner's jury were present. The only person missing was the murderer. We were there for an hour and listened to the evidence presented by the police and the medical examiner. The jurors deliberated over evidence and declared what we already knew; that Momma's death was indeed murder at the hands of an unknown assailant.

Funerals and Memorial Services

There is no wrong or right way to have a funeral or memorial service. Trust your instincts. The time surrounding a murder is confusing and complicated. You will have many feelings. The funeral or memorial service provides an opportunity for family, friends and community to offer support and sympathy and to say good-bye to the dead person. The warmth and closeness that is experienced during this time may help in the long aftermath of homicide.

In some large urban areas a few funeral directors solicit clients. Some wait around the medical examiner's facility and approach prospective clients. They also try to gain information about the survivor's address. A funeral director actually followed my father home to offer us a cut-rate funeral for my mother. But my family had been using the same funeral director for forty years, and his services were the ones we used.

Don't be intimidated. You do have control over what happens to you and your deceased loved one's body. And remember, for most families the funeral director is among the most supportive persons.

The Criminal Justice Process

If a suspect is arrested, the criminal justice process will begin. This means more contact with the police and news media. It means contact with a district attorney, judge, possibly a jury, and a victims assistance counselor. After the arrest, the defendant is arraigned and bail is or is not set. Many murderers are not allowed out on bail. A preliminary hearing is held. At this point the district attorney's office has to show that a crime/murder has happened and that enough evidence exists to hold a trial.

Next a pre-trial arraignment will take place. Although survivors may attend the preliminary hearing, they do not attend the pre-trial arraignment. During this period, the defense and district attorneys file motions, gather facts and maybe even plea bargain. Plea bargaining means a suspect pleads guilty to a lesser charge in order to save court expense and time and stress of a trial. If a suspect pleads guilty, there will be no court trial. If a murder trial takes place, the survivors should be notified. This notification may come from the district attorney's office, homicide investigator or from a victim assistance program. If you are worried about being forgotten and not notified, make sure you have a contact in the district attorney's office or in the victim assistance program. Call often.

The district attorney's job is to gather evidence for the trial and represent the people. Many survivors say that the assistant district attorneys prosecuting the case were compassionate and competent. They kept the survivors abreast of changes in court schedules and accompanied them to the courtroom. Another person on the scene is the crime victim assistance counselor.

Crime Victims Assistance Programs

Since the late 60's and early 70's, crime victims assistance programs have been established in almost every state. These professionals have helped to bring the plight of all crime victims and survivors of murder victims to the public eye. They have helped lobby for laws to assist crime victims. These counselors provide court accompanyment services for you and assist in applying for crime victim compensation. They also act as the victim's advocate whenever necessary and will help you write a victim's impact statement.

Victim's Impact Statement

The victim's impact statement is a written paper detailing the emotional, financial and physical cost that the murder has had on the victim's survivors. The letter is given to the judge prior to sentencing the convicted person.

Victim Compensation

You may be able to file an application for compensation for out-of-pocket expenses you paid following your loved one's murder. Most states have a Crime Victims Compensation Board. The rules governing each board may vary from state to state. Compensation is paid for uninsured medical expenses, counseling, loss of support, cash loss benefits, and funeral expenses. However, there are stipulations to a survivor receiving this money. The murder victim must be deemed innocent, to receive counseling payments you must have lived in the house with the victim, you must be a parent, child, sibling or spouse. Other eligibility requirements are:

The crime must be reported within 72 hours.

The survivors must cooperate with the law.

Expenses must be documented: records must be kept.

The claim must be filed within a year.

The applicant cannot live in the same house as the offender at the end of the trial.

The minimum loss set by the state has been met.

Many survivors, especially African-Americans have been dissatisfied with the Crime Victims Compensation Boards. They feel victimized and are angry at having to prove that their loved ones were innocent. One mother reported filing for compensation and being turned down. The board denied her claim on the grounds that her son had used drugs. She refiled after she proved this was not true. The board turned her down a second time on he grounds that her son lived at another residence. She is now refiling because her son was living at home and killed at a friend's house.

If you have a complaint about the way you are treated, check with your local victims assistance agency. If you do not know where it is located, ask your district attorney's office or the police.

Moving Down The Path - Part II

The Homicide Bereavement Cycle

The Slaying of Marcus

Anthony (11), Malcom (6), and Marcus (5) were brothers, playmates and buddies. Marcus had chicken pox during the second week of July and had to stay in the house. On Sunday he was feeling better, so when Grandma invited the boys to spend the night at her house, he wanted to go! They all wanted a pajama party at Grandma's house. They pleaded and begged and finally their mother, Rochelle, said yes. She dressed Marcus quickly, gave him a quick good-bye kiss, then told the boys, *Your father and I will pick you up after work tomorrow.*

Monday was hot. Rochelle and Anthony Yates left for work by 6:00 a.m. At lunch time, Rochelle called her mother to check on her sons and was told they were playing outside. Later that afternoon Marcus, Malcom, and Anthony went with their young aunts and uncles to a neighborhood grocery store to buy candy. Children gathered there daily to buy goodies and play video games. While the little boys were in the store, two young men came in and began to argue. One of the men called the other a homosexual. The man angrily left the store and came back with a gun. Both men began to shoot at each other. The children were scared and panicked. They began to run for cover. Everyone found a hiding place except the younger children. Malcom was shot in the leg. Marcus was shot in the side of the head. Anthony ran to his younger brother and placed his finger in the hole to try to stop the bleeding.

Police and ambulances arrived. The children were in shock, crying and trying to describe what had happened. In the ambulance rushing to the hospital Malcom, in pain from the gunshot wound in his leg, watched his baby brother. He told his mother, *I saw blood coming out of his eyes and ears. I saw life going out of my brother's face. I wanted to help him and there was nothing I could do.*

The Family's Story

Malcom was told by his parents that his brother and buddy, Marcus, had died. Because he was in the hospital, Malcom was unable to attend the funeral. His parents took him to the cemetery when he was released from the hospital. At first, Malcom did not believe his brother was dead. He tried to keep Marcus alive. He told his mother, *Marcus talks to me in my head and helps me with my homework.* He did not want anyone to forget that Marcus had lived. Malcom asked that the family have a birthday cake for Marcus' birthday the next year. Although Anthony did attend the funeral, he also pretended his brother was not dead. He fantasized that Marcus was away in Georgia visiting his uncle. Both brothers openly admitted it was hard to accept their younger brother's violent death.

Rochelle said of that day, *Upon reaching my mother's house my husband, Tony, and I saw that the street was blocked off by police. There were people standing all over the streets. I said, 'there they go again'.* Rochelle was talking about people who made trouble in her mother's neighborhood. As Tony parked the car, Rochelle realized that none of her children had run to greet them as they usually did.

Suddenly, I felt a cold chill go up my spine, Rochelle said. Tony, a Vietnam veteran, had told her about a premonition he had earlier. *I had strange feelings that I was going to be shot and killed by a sniper while sitting in traffic. This thought has been with me all day.*

Finally, Rochelle spotted Anthony. *Mom! Marcus and Malcom were taken to the hospital. They were shot!* he said. Tony and Rochelle tried to calm him down and learn what had happened. There was too much confusion and the unhurt children were crying in the background. She went to the police officer standing in front of the store and asked, *What hospital were our children taken to?* The police escorted them to the hospital. A trauma unit worker rushed the family into the waiting area. Soon Rochelle and Tony were taken in to see their sons. *When we came into the emergency room, my heart stopped. My baby had been shot in the right temple.* Rochelle said. She felt as if she were having a nightmare and could not wake up. *Not in my wildest imagination did I ever think that I would be confronted with my baby being a murder victim and almost losing my other two sons.*

The family was torn apart by Marcus' unexpected, violent death. Tony said, *After fighting in Vietnam, I never thought I would have to be afraid of my sons dying on American streets.* As the family tried to deal with individual feelings, their anger would flair out at one another. Silent pain and suffering was destroying their family. Anthony and Malcom were becoming confrontive and defensive in school. The boys, A/B students prior to the murder, were failing. Rochelle learned a month after Marcus' death that she was pregnant. She angrily said, *Is God trying to replace my son?* Newspaper reporters wrote about the family constantly. There was not a moment's peace.

Rochelle and Tony spent a lot of time at marches, demonstrations and making television appearances. All their activities were around fighting the drug environment that had killed Marcus. Rochelle knew her family was drifting apart. She was too exhausted to care. In fact, she didn't want to care too much. She feared her other children might also be taken from her by sudden death.

Eventually, she and the boys found the Homicide Bereavement Center. They soon learned that although their grief was unique, other families at the center could identify with their pain and sorrow. They also discovered that many of the families were law-abiding citizens who shared some of the same life dreams and accomplishments. The Yates family learned that they were not alone.

Homicide Bereavement

Many death educators and counselors view the bereavement process as a series of stages or phases the grieved survivors must go through. However, I prefer to characterize the homicide bereavement process as cyclical. It comes in cycles as survivors are forced to relive the murder over and over again at recurring periods, usually until the trial is completed. It is also cyclical grief due to the wide fluctuations of emotions which you may feel when faced by a wide variety of external events.

The homicide bereavement process consists of three cycles: crisis, conflict and commencement. These cycles are not distinct. You may experience and identify feelings from all cycles at once. What is important is that you are able to begin to understand why you act, feel and think the way you do. This new knowledge about your actions, emotions and thoughts can help you take charge and gain control.

HOMICIDE GRIEF EXPERIENCE

CRISIS *(Challenge/Acceptance)*	CONFLICT *(Confrontation/Adjustment)*	COMMENCEMENT *(Change/Adaptation)*

CRISIS	CONFLICT	COMMENCEMENT
Death Notification	Mourning Delayed	Trial Ends
Autopsy		Holiday Blues
Identify Victim	Arrest	Closure on Business
Police Investigation	Preliminary Hearing	Mourning
Media Reports	Arraignments	Group Support
Funeral/Burial	Homicide Trial	Healing
Mourning Begins		Anniversaries
	No Arrest	
	Unsolved Murder	
Shock (Numbness)	Unfinished Business	Focus on the Living
Denial (Questioning)		Pleasant Memories
Anger and Rage	Acquittal	Happy Days
Revenge	Conviction	New Growth
Fear	Sentencing	Gradual Change
Anxiety		Self Oriented Thoughts
Victim Centered Preoccupation	Victim Impact Statement	Longing
Sleep Problems		Relief
Appetite Changes		
	Guilt	
	Despair	
	Betrayal	
	Powerlessness	
	Abandonment	
	Bitter	

HOMICIDE GRIEF CYCLE

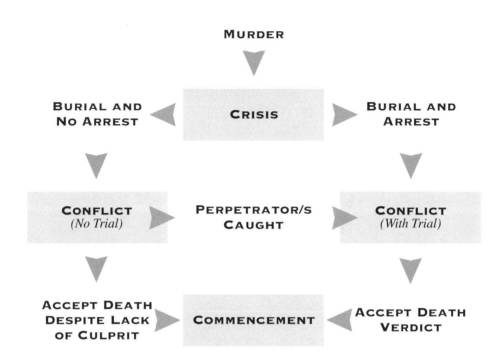

The Crisis Cycle

This is the cycle of loss. The murder victim is dead and you become the living victim in murder's aftermath. Your victimization begins with notification of the murder. No matter how many other deaths or losses you have experienced, this one will be different. Vastly different. You have to accept two shocks: the death and the homicide. How did you feel? Angry, numb, flushed, wanting revenge? Did you scream? Fight? Faint? It doesn't matter. Whatever you felt, said or did was alright. This was the start of your crisis cycle. Some people panic, some perform and some pass out. No two people say or do the same things. You were experiencing shock.

At this point, like Malcom, you may say that the homicide did not take place and deny the whole event. Shock is a physical phenomenon which provides you with a trauma absorber. It helps your body and emotions adjust to the murder until you are able to accept it. Shock neutralizes your senses for a short while. It gives you time to sort out your feelings and thoughts. You are able to do things you probably never thought you could ever face.

During your crisis cycle, you can only think and wonder about how such a loss could happen. At times, you may have felt over-whelmed by the comings and goings of the police, reporters, and friends. Although you wanted company and compassion, there were times when you wanted some peace and privacy. Rochelle was dismayed by the way the news media went after them to get a story. She was touted as a heroine when all she wanted to do was have her little boy back. She knew that people wanted her to be brave and not share her real pain. She was so brave she became depressed.

For some of you, the insensitivity and public intrusion into your life is too much. You may transfer your anger from the murderer to those nearest you: family, friends, the police or the media. Do not feel ashamed. Anyone who really cares about you knows you were in shock and suffering. The only thing you could have coped with during this cycle was mourning your tragic loss.

If you are at this stage of grief, remember, first things first. Bury the dead. At this point you are the living victim. Your family members and friends must face this tragedy and experience the trauma. You are the one who has been violated and overwhelmed.

Do whatever you need to do within legal boundaries to feel the pain:
> Cry all you want.
> Do not allow others to determine how you should grieve.
> Trust your emotions; they will not lead you astray.
> Avoid people who want to take control of your life.
> Be with those who allow you to be yourself.

There are no quick steps or short cuts to getting through this period. You simply must go through the crisis cycle at your own pace and timing.

It's not easy, but here are some practical tips to help you as you meet the demands of this period.

Try not to do too much by yourself.

Ask a friend or family member to assist you during the funeral and burial-planning process.

You do not have to be brave or strong. Although it may seem impossible, get plenty of rest. Burying a loved one is exhausting work.

Don't assume anything. Ask questions about any issues, situation or technique you didn't or don't understand.

Forgive yourself and others. You may have been unkind or felt that others were especially rude to you or your loved ones. The period between death notification and the burial is complex and confusing. Anything done or said during this time should be excused. You and your loved ones are only human. Wounded individuals are not on their best behavior.

A companion to forgiveness is forgetting. Forget about all the things you failed to remember. Even under the best circumstances, the death of a loved one impairs our ability to think clearly. Maybe you didn't find the blue tie you wanted him to be buried in. You did the best under the most traumatic and stressful circumstances. You don't deserve a self-inflicted guilt trip.

Conflict Cycle

This is the law enforcement and/or criminal justice cycle. At this point, you are a survivor who has started to cope with an awful reality-- someone you loved has been murdered. The funeral, burial, or cremation are completed. The visitors are gone. You may have returned to work or school. Life goes on for distant relatives, friends and neighbors. This cycle begins when the criminal justice process starts and is called "conflict" because your actions and emotions are wrapped around what happens during that process. Many of you put your anger and need for vengeance on hold in the crisis cycle. You expect the legal process to address your needs and believe you will feel better after the trial.

Oh, but the wheels of justice grind slowly. You may have become frustrated with the justice system and given up. You may have thought the trial would never take place. And, because it takes so long for some of your loved ones' cases to come to trial, you may have already started feeling better. Then the trial started and you were catapulted back into active grief.

The conflict during this cycle can come from several possible realizations. You may have come to realize that:
1. the District Attorney was representing the state, not you or your deceased loved one.
2. the murderer had no remorse for the crime.
3. the defense attorney was allowed to prosecute your deceased loved one as a method of defense.
4. you had no rights and were only an observer at the trial.

If you or someone you know is at this cycle of bereavement, the rules and regulations that govern the smooth operation of the criminal justice process are difficult to grasp. You were probably shocked and angered at some of the things you learned in court and you were not satisfied. You may have entered the courtroom thinking the trial and verdict would help your pain and suffering. In most cases, it does not. The trial is a sad reminder of your loved one's tragic and traumatic death.

During the trial you are a survivor because you learned how to cope with the things you cannot change. At the court, a Crime Victims Assistance counselor should be assisting you. This person will help you understand the criminal justice process, as well as encourage you to manage your emotions and your need to strike out at the murderer. Some days you will be enraged. Other days you will be sad. Some days you will feel vindicated. It is a period of conflict because your emotions may range from high to low from hour to hour and day to day.

Marcus' family was furious because after waiting more than 18 months for the murder trial, the judge ordered that they would not be allowed to attend. He felt the parent's presence in the court room would influence their children's testimony. So Rochelle and Tony were told they could not hear Anthony and Malcom testify. Imagine burying your murdered love one but told you can not attend the murder trial. However, with the help of other victims and the news media, the Yates protested the decision. Finally, after a stern warning from the judge not to do anything that could influence the jury or jeopardize the court proceeding, Rochelle and Anthony were allowed in the courtroom.

Since it takes so long for some cases to be prosecuted, you may have found ways to survive and start to grieve the loss. However, from the pre-trial hearings to the final proceedings your methods of survival and grieving are constantly delayed or interrupted. You may find yourself forced back to the crisis cycle where you are just able to make it from moment to moment. This is difficult. Just when you think your pain is lessening , it gets worse.

Several things will help you during the conflict cycle:

Do not expect the criminal justice process to meet your emotional needs. The judicial process' only objectives are to insure the smooth running and fair administration of the legal process.

Don't personalize every remark said about your loved one. It is the defense attorney's job to represent his or her client, the accused murderer. Whatever the defense attorney says about your loved one does not change the relationship you shared.

Contact your local Crime Victims Assistance professional and ask for help.This will enable you to understand the judicial process and receive constant reassurance and support. Keep all receipts for expenses that were not covered by medical or life insurance. This will help you in filing for crime victim compensation. Ask the counselor to guide you in writing a victim's impact statement. The court won't be able to use it in capital cases, but writing it will help you to focus on and understand your own feelings.

Leave the courtroom if you feel overwhelmed and out of control. You don't want to be the source of a mistrial or misdirected verdict. In fact, if you don't want to attend the trial at all, it's okay.

Use a written statement when talking to the news media. If you're uncomfortable use a spokesperson at press conferences.

Don't expect to experience satisfaction after the verdict.

Initially, Belinda was pleased with the death sentence given to her son's murderer. Yet, she now admits it only met a fleeting need.

The end of this cycle occurs when the trial is completely over and the defendant has been convicted, sentenced, imprisoned or executed. However, there are times when trials end in an acquittal. If the judicial decision seems too lenient or the defendant was acquitted, you may feel cheated and further victimized. Marcus' family felt that the life sentences given the two men responsible for his death were too easy. Neither Marcus' nor James' family was helped emotionally by the judicial process. They still needed help to resolve their grief.

When the trial is over, put it behind you. You can't change anything about the judicial proceedings. After the convicted has been sentenced, you have a right to be notified when he or she comes up for parole. You can write a victim's impact statement or speak at the parole hearing. I believe it is important to do what makes you feel best. Trust yourself.

The crisis and conflict cycles are actually a part of your grief process. For many survivors, it is easier to accept the loss than the method of dying. You probably have concerns about your loved one's feelings at the time of the murder. You want to know how much fear, pain and suffering there was. You probably felt a sense of relief if the coroner's report revealed that death was instant. Regardless of what happened, it is imperative for you to both face and accept the death and adjust to the murder. Then you can advance to the final cycle.

The Commencement Cycle

This final cycle of grief is signaled by your own willingness to mourn. At the start of this cycle, you are still a survivor. You are still making adjustments to your sudden loss. You realize that enough time has gone by and you want to reorganize your life. You start to remember that before the murder you had dreams and plans. You want your dreams to come true, but the reality of murder has altered the way you act, feel, and think. As I said, Momma's murder used to live within me. But when I reached this cycle, I was ready to change and develop from my experience. My life became more important to me than the cause of Momma's death. When you feel this way, you're ready to enter the commencement cycle.

There are two major goals which must take place in the commencement cycle: **grief resolution and social reorganization.** William J. Worden, (*Grief Counseling and Grief Therapy*) says there are four tasks in mourning:
Accepting the reality of the loss.
Experiencing the pain of the loss.
Adjusting to an environment with the deceased missing.
Withdrawing emotional energy from the deceased and reinvesting it into other relationships and activities.
During the crisis and conflict cycle you were probably forced in one way or another to accept and experience the horrendous reality and pain of losing a loved one to homicidal death. Therefore, the final two tasks will be met when you are able to develop in several ways. You need to be able to:
function in the world,
transfer your feelings and energy,
live in the present,
think of your loved one with pleasant memories and feelings.

To function in the world - you are able to meet the demands of each day without feeling overly stressed. You experience days when you don't concentrate on or think about the deceased. After resolving her grief, Belinda was able to return to managing her household. Rochelle began to encourage her children and husband to grieve Marcus' death and work together to rebuild their family life.

To transfer feelings and energy - you begin to think about and care for your living loved ones more than you concentrate on your feelings for your dead family member. In other words, you spend more time and energy on those who are alive. You give away the victim's clothing and other personal articles. Yes, you keep things that are special, but certain belongings, pictures and other momentos become secure in a special place in your home and your heart.

To live in the present - even though everyone's grief clock is different. You know it's time to move on when the trial is over or you simply are tired of grieving. When Rochelle's and Belinda's children started to behave in ways that were displeasing, these mothers knew it was time to live for today. There was no trial in my mother's case, but I knew it was time when I was tired of carrying the burden of grief. Trust yourself, go with your feelings.

Thinking about your loved one - who first of all was an important part of your life, is natural and normal. Death is only an end to physical existence. Your loved one lives in the special times you shared. It's really alright and even great to remember those times. Some of your thoughts may cause sadness, but others will make you laugh and or feel joy. Meeting the goal of grief resolution happens by:

talking about your loss with those who want to listen,

believing it is okay to move on with your life,

accepting that you could not change circumstances surrounding the murder.

Your life has been irrevocably changed. But your life is not over or destroyed; it is altered. Someone you love is no longer alive and present. Two pertinent concepts to remember are that no two persons will grieve in the same way, not even identical twins; and recovery lengths will vary. It may take as little as two years to reach grief resolution. For some it may be four to seven years. The most important thing you can do is embrace your grief and get through it.

The other task of the commencement cycle is social reorganization. Murder does change the way you view life, but that view can be better, more acute and frightfully realistic. You know social reorganization is occurring when you want to spend less time alone and have more contact with your peers. You may find that you return to organizations you left after the murder. You may want to become involved in activities that support victims and fight crime. Once you have reorganized your social life, you may start living again and start to consider what new directions may be ahead for you.

31

Variables Which May Alter Bereavement

While the pattern of homicide bereavement is discernible and unique, no two grief styles will be identical. There are several things which influence the cycles of homicide bereavement:

the type of homicide,

the survivor's role and relationship to the victim,

the family's relationship after the loss,

the societal response to the survivors after the murder.

Belinda's son's body was mutilated. It was hard for her to accept that what she saw in the casket was her son. Rochelle, too, admits that her son did not look like himself. However, in my case it was the fact that my mother looked so healthy. I found it hard to accept that she had died from a bullet wound. Murders that involve savagery, rape, mutilation, torture or other horrors can naturally cause you to have a complicated period of grief.

Your role as a spouse, parent, child, sibling or other family member or friend may also influence the style of your grief. Family members may have to learn not to put pressure on each other to grieve a certain way or within a specific time frame. Rochelle was very angry at her family. She felt that some were not showing enough grief while others were expressing too much. Belinda, on the other hand, felt that nobody within her family could be feeling what she was experiencing. Many did not share their grief at all.

The most vocal survivors are the parents of murdered children, especially mothers. If you are a parent, you feel extremely violated when a child is murdered. You feel guilty about not being able to protect your child. You may think you've failed your child. Belinda said, *God gave me this life to take care of and I failed.* Your major grief task is to accept that **you are not responsible for your child's death.** Belinda felt guilty because she thought her warning to James about his friendships was somehow a death wish. Rochelle thought if she had kept Marcus home and sent him to school he would still be alive. I often thought that if I had lived at home I could have helped save Momma's life. We all have real or imagined guilt. But remember, no amount of wishful thinking will change the events. If you could do that, then your loved one would not be dead.

Next to parents, spouses are most vocal about homicidal loss. If you are a spouse, you may have lost a lover, a provider, household manager, co-parent and best friend. A lot of your major role identification changed with the death: spouse to widow/widower, single parent and head of the household. Like the mothers, wives seem to receive attention, support and compassion from others.

After mourning their losses, I have found that mothers and wives are often the motivation behind forcing other family members to address their own grief. After completing the grief process, Rochelle and Belinda shared the progress they had made with their husbands and helped encourage their children to mourn. I have shared my progress with my siblings. A major grief task for spouses and parents is to try to include other family members, especially their children in the grief process.

Men - fathers, husbands, sons and brothers find it hard to grieve because of their perceived role in society as strong and unwavering. As a man, you may feel it is unmanly to cry or express pain and suffering. People expect you to bear everybody else's burden and provide a shoulder to lean on. But you are human and loved your deceased relative or friend. You don't have to carry the family's grief. Just carry your own and share with others. Your guilt is often focused on the fact that you feel you should have protected and kept your wife or child or sibling from being murdered.

The role changes may also mean fathers find themselves suddenly having to take care of household chores and learning how to do child care management. Give yourself time. You may want to find a support group for men. Remember, you could not change the circumstances of your loss. If you need help with children, ask for it.

Children face a difficult process because the adult world often does not understand or respect their right to grieve. Regardless of their ages, children and siblings of murdered relatives develop a feeling of being unprotected and vulnerable. If you are the child related to a murder victim, you may feel competitive with the dead sibling. Mom and Dad may be so grieved that they are not providing you the attention you need and want.

Malcom came to every bereavement meeting with his mother. He made his presence known. He was so verbal about his grief that at some meetings this seven-year-old motivated adults to talk about their pain. Children need to be included in every cycle of the grief process. Let them help plan the funeral, take them to grief sessions and encourage them to help in celebrating the life of your loved one.

Distant relatives and are also survivors. Often you will not be considered true mourners or real survivors although you may have been closer to the victim than immediate family members. Do not hide your grief. Be supportive to family members but also stress that you are there to mourn the death. Spend time listening and sharing your mutual grief. It is all right for you, too, to attend a grief support group.

Another issue that affects survivors of murder victims is social isolation. Survivors often feel isolated because people seem to avoid them. Aside from the myths we talked about there are other reasons why you may experience social isolation:
People are afraid that your loss may happen to them.
They avoid you to protect their lives and families.
They do not know the enormity of your loss and suffering.
They do not know what to say or how to comfort you.
They are not aware that they are adding to the trauma and victimization you already experienced.

Strengthening Relationships

Because of the mode of death, people competing to be the chief mourner and the social isolation, some families and friendships do break up following homicidal loss. The stress and strain of this death may have weakened your family structure and friendships. To maintain and strengthen your relationships during bereavement and grief, consider the five following suggestions:
Talk to your loved ones and friends about what each of you have experienced as a result of your mutual loss.
Respect each other's mourning practices. Each of you is unique, therefore, your expression of pain and suffering will vary.
Resist the temptation to compete with each other or to be the chief mourner. Remember, each family member or friend shared a special role and relationship to the deceased.
Rebuild your life and relationships moment by moment with the understanding that someone you love was killed and will never return. Take small steps to renew yourself and restore old acquaintances.
Work with your loved ones to establish an annual celebration of life to commemorate the deceased's life.

The Unending Cycle of Pain - Complicated Grief

Complicated grieving arises when you are unable to mourn, grieve too long, or cannot reach grief resolution. Four situations which often complicate the bereavement process are:
A belief that justice was not carried out.
An unsolved murder
A multiple murder
A murder-suicide

Unfair Justice

It was a hot summer night. Martin decided to visit his girlfriend. As he was walking down a quiet city street, he saw a friend approaching him. The friend swung out at him, said *Hey Man!* and stabbed him in the chest. Martin began to run and stagger. Two policemen saw him and ran to him. He said, *My friend just stabbed me.* The policemen took him to the nearest hospital. Martin had lost a massive amount of blood and his lungs had collapsed. He died shortly after arriving at the emergency room. He was 17 years old. His murderer, another teenager, was high on drugs and did not realize what he had done. The murderer was sentenced to a short jail term and was out of prison in two years. Martin's family was outraged and devastated. They felt that the judicial system had betrayed them.

Prolonged Grief

Prolonged grief occurs when, like Martin's family, you become stuck in one cycle of bereavement. You may feel as if your whole life is stuck. Martin's family could only focus on their anger. Instead of being angry at the murderer for killing Martin, they were angry at the judicial system for not avenging the loss in a manner acceptable to them. They thought the justice system was a joke.

Prolonged grief separates family members from those with whom they are angry. It breaks down the family's relationship to each other. Martin's family members grew apart. Since they seemed unable to help one another, each family member found ways to cope with the violent death. A few years after his death, Martin's parent's divorced and his father left the entire family.

Over a long period of time, prolonged grieving becomes un-bearable. You may find you need relief from the depression and sadness. Martin's family member's lifestyles suffered. His mother and a couple of his siblings became addicted to either alcohol or drugs. Eventually, his mother lost control of the house, the children and was terminated from her job at a local department store.

Today, many years after Martin's death, his family still has not resolved or accepted their loss. To handle their grief this family seldom sees each other and Martin is seldom, if ever, spoken of by his loved ones.

Unsolved Homicide

Ann was a 36-year-old widowed mother of three children: two sons and a daughter. She lived in a quiet suburban town. One Friday afternoon, when her children arrived home from school, they found Ann strangled to death. She was lying on the floor with an extension cord around her neck. The house was a wreck, furniture was overturned, household items and jewelry were missing, and her purse was stolen. There were signs that she struggled with her murderer. The police checked every lead for months. A community fund offered a reward for information which would lead to the capture of the killer. Nothing worked. The murderer's identity was never discovered.

Ann's Children

During the week of the funeral, Ann's best friend, Karen, stayed at the house with the children. Because Ann had no immediate family members other than her minor children, Karen planned the funeral. She did not include the children in the planning and 5-year-old Amy was not allowed to attend the service. Karen felt she was too young. Karen adopted Amy and 8-year-old Tad, but she did not want to take a 15-year-old. Ann's oldest son, Jack, was placed in a group home. None of the children were ever asked what they wanted to do. They lost their mother, a home and each other.

Two years after Ann's death, Jack had only been allowed to visit his siblings four times. He felt abandoned, isolated and thought about his mother all the time. He slept with the light on at night and hid a knife under his pillow. Amy and Tad also slept with a night light. Amy had nightmares at least three times a week. She thought someone was going to kill her, too. Amy told Ann that she saw her mother some nights. Tad was a discipline problem. He fought all the time and skipped school. The young children cried for their brother and waited for Jack to become 18. They longed to be together and hoped on his birthday he could become their guardian.

The children never received bereavement or grief therapy. There were no peer support groups available for them. And, since the murder was never solved, Ann's children were fearful that the murderer would come back and kill them. They felt immense pain and sorrow; yet they did not know what to do with their grief. The adults had told them they would get over their mother's death. Each child knew years later that they had not "gotten over it."

Unresolved Grief

If the case remains unsolved this will complicate the bereavement process in several ways.

Not having a trial short-circuits the conflict cycle because there is no identifiable focus for your anger. As a result, your anger is often displaced. You may be angry at the police and believe they did not try to solve the case. I felt that way and so did many in my family. After two weeks, we knew Momma's death would never be solved. We said the police aren't going to try too hard because one dead black person was one less black person to care about. And after all these years, we doubt that our mother's murder will ever be solved.

Unresolved murder also short circuits the commencement cycle because of unfinished business. Like my grandmother, you may feel you can never be healed until the murderer is caught and prosecuted. My grandmother, Julia Chisolm, once said to me, *Wanda, I don't want to die without finding out who killed her. I pray that God will let me know who shot my daughter. I won't feel good again until I know why my Juanita was murdered. It just didn't make sense.* When I stood over my grandmother's casket on February 5, 1990, a week before the 18th anniversary of Momma's death, I said to myself, *Grandma Julia, you died not knowing the truth. But now you are in eternity where the truth and being with your daughter again will set you free.*

Unresolved grief means that there is no end to your grief or pain. Emotions may fluctuate back and forth. Some days you feel good and other days you feel depressed. On special days such as anniversaries and birthdays your grief is intensified. The general rule is that your bad days are likely to outnumber your good ones.

Murder-Suicide

Jake had visions and heard voices regularly. His wife, Joan, was planning to leave him. One Saturday morning, Jake shot his wife in the heart and drowned both of his children. Then Jake shot himself in the head and died. A neighbor who heard the shots called the police.

Jake and Joan's Families

Jake and Joan's parents and siblings were devastated. Joan's family was grieved and enraged. They forbade Jake's family from attending the funeral of the children and Joan. They blamed them for Jake's insane behavior and they did not attend Jake's funeral. Jake's family could not understand how Joan's family could be angry with them. They felt cheated and were angry at Joan's family for not allowing them to attend their daughter-in-law's and grandchildren's funeral. Although Joan's family eventually stopped blaming Jake's family and apologized for their behavior during the early cycle of bereavement, the two families' relationship was destroyed. Both families were so full of anger and guilt that neither was able to resolve their conflict or grieve the losses.

Aborted Grief

Aborted grief is "cut-off grief". Something within your environment stopped your grief.

One factor which may cause grief to be aborted is the judicial process. The murderer may have been found innocent or the sentence may have seemed too lenient. Another cause of aborted grief is social neglect. Society does not accept or sanction the survivor's right to grieve. You may feel pressured to bounce back into circulation or find that no one thinks you should grieve. This happens quite often with children and to the relatives in a suicide-murder or double murder. Whatever the reason may be, you know that you have not grieved your loss. You know that something cut-off your grief. Just because your grief has been interrupted does not mean you stop feeling sad. It means you don't want or know how to share with others what you are experiencing.

I felt from the moment I learned of Momma's death that I was supposed to be brave. And believe me, my siblings and I were brave!

We tried not to cry and we put on a front for all the well-wishers and consolers. It was five years before anyone validated my right to mourn a woman I had loved all my life. Maybe you can or cannot identify with this experience. But you do know when your reaction to the loss feels unnatural.

Reach inside yourself and embrace your pain. Then reach out and share with another survivor or a therapist who can help you resolve your grief and relieve the suffering. You may feel as I did and reaching the source of your pain and suffering may be difficult, but it is not impossible. Just know this: a time period longer than a year is too long not to feel the pain and express your grief.

Homicide Stress Syndrome

If your grief remains aborted, prolonged or unresolved, you may experience a negative build-up of stress. Over a period of time, you could experience post-traumatic stress disorder.

Post-traumatic stress is a mental health diagnosis which classifies the long-term impact of psychological trauma. You have probably heard about this as it relates to Vietnam veterans. In the case of homicidal loss, it means survivors of murder victims may have left-over stress and trauma reactions years after the actual homicide. This is not an unusual occurrence because of the nature of the loss, judicial process, social isolation and lack of adequate grief services.

I call the post-traumatic stress associated with murder *homicide stress syndrome* because the reaction is directly related to the homicidal death of your family member or friend. Murder is a brutal, traumatic loss which produces emotional scarring. As we can see with Ann's children, they were fearful and had lost everything. Homicidal loss produces scars that time alone will not eliminate.

It is important to highlight the fact that homicide stress syndrome is not unusual following the murder of someone you love. The reaction may result from witnessing the actual crime. It's a pretty tough and helpless experience to see a loved one killed right before your eyes, especially if you are a child. You suffer many losses at once: your loved one, a sense of safety, trust, and a belief in humanity. Homicide stress syndrome is an unending cycle of pain and suffering. You find that you never reach grief resolution or social reorganization. In essence, you cannot move into the commencement cycle.

Homicide stress syndrome is a combination of reactions which occur regularly over a period of time and is identifiable in three ways:
In some way, you repeatedly re-experience the murder.
You find ways to deny that you feel or think about the murder.
You are unable to maintain your personal stability.

Repeatedly re-experiencing the murder may take the form of day visions or nightmares in which the murder is visualized. There is a need to constantly describe the murder over and over again to anyone who will listen. Denial of feelings and thoughts associated with the murder may surface through forgetfulness, self-isolation, and regression.

Belinda admits, *For over a year, I did not remember seeing my son's face at the morgue. I could only see the diamond earring in his ear.* Many children return to thumb sucking or sleeping with a light on. Ann's children all needed a light in order to fall asleep. While all these reactions are absolutely normal for some time after the death, if they continue for more than a year, you may be seeing a stress syndrome.

An inability to maintain your personal stability may be viewed in several ways.
The family begins to breakdown.
Social life deteriorates.
There is sorrow without relief.
There is drug, alcohol or food addictions.
Phobias occur.
You experience either insomnia or excessive sleeping.

While thoughts of suicide and homicide are normal in grief, if they continue - get help. You may also find that you are verbally or physically abusive to loved ones. These behaviors were not present prior to the homicide. You are not going crazy. These are normal reactions. Our concern comes if they continue for a prolonged period of time.

Homicide stress syndrome is not a signal that you have not accepted your loss or gone through the first cycle of homicide bereavement. It is a sign that your grief was sidetracked. You have not completed the final tasks of mourning and the grief is unresolved.

Keep six things in mind as it relates to yourself and society:

You have a right to mourn the loss.

People do care; they just don't understand murder and don't always know how to address the grief you feel.

The police do care about solving the crime.

You have a right to seek professional support from a qualified bereavement therapist.

It will probably help to join a support group for survivors of murder victims. It helps to be with others who understand and have experienced the same type of loss.

If you have noticed any of the signals described in this chapter, don't try to diagnose yourself. Seek professional help and intervention.

The Light At The End Of The Tunnel - Part III
Celebrating Their Lives

The Assassination of Michael

In November after midnight, Michael had gone off duty from his job as a Cook County Deputy Sheriff. Michael was hungry. He stopped at a local restaurant and purchased chicken to take home and eat. While he was waiting, three young men began harassing customers and making a disturbance. Michael produced his badge and asked the young men to leave the facility without any trouble. They left, seemingly peacefully.

After Michael received his order, he left the restaurant. As he was walking toward his car, two of the young men jumped him from behind and held his arms. The third took Michael's gun from his holster, placed it to Mike's head and shot him. He fell down and died instantly, as his blood and brains spilled to the ground.

Michael's death was big news because he was a member of the law-enforcement community. It was especially sad news to me because he was my brother-in-law. The funeral was so crowded that it was difficult for some family members and friends to find a parking space. My sister and the immediate family received immense emotional and social support because of Mike's status. He will be remembered as a slain hero.

Celebrating Good Works

As I was preparing to write this chapter, I read an article by Chuck Stone, a writer for the *Philadelphia Daily News*. He contrasted the vast differences in his initial grief following the death of Rev. Adam Clayton Powell and the murder of Dr. Martin Luther King, Jr. With the death of Rev. Powell, Chuck felt a sense of nostalgia. With the slaying of Dr. King, he felt nothing but sadness. His response to the murder of a beloved friend was no surprise to me. But as I read on, Mr. Stone made a statement that captured the essence of this chapter. To paraphrase: *Americans would remember King's death by celebrating his transforming good works.*

Most of our holidays and holy days are times to celebrate the transforming good works of persons whose acts of courage have advanced humanity. These celebrations allow public and private groups an opportunity to remember and testify about the nature of someone's contributions.

Let's review some of these occasions. Christians celebrate the transforming works of Jesus at Easter and Christmas. Passover permits the Jewish community to commemorate God's protection of Israel's first born during the night when the Angel of Death took the lives of Egyptian babies. President's Day honors the works of all our American presidents. Veteran's day pays honor to both the living and dead veteran. The list is endless. Celebrating the transforming good works of the deceased is our way of remembering our dead and sharing our history. I believe an important sign that your grief has been resolved is your ability to set aside specific times during the year when you choose to commemorate and celebrate the transforming good works of your deceased loved one's life.

You might say, *Well he wasn't a police officer, mayor, civil rights activist or president.* In fact, he may have died as a result of a fight or drugs. She may have been an infant or illiterate. These things don't matter. Your loved one was an important person in your life. You loved him, and he loved you. As family members and friends, you have a right to set aside time to share with others what was contributed to your life.

The Benefits of Celebrating Life

We survivors of murder victims are among some of the most famous people in the world. Coretta Scott King, Charles Evers, Caroline Kennedy, Ethel Kennedy, the Chaneys, the Ghandis, the Sadats and Malcom X's family members are all survivors of murder victims. You have as much right as celebrity survivors to commemorate a deceased person's life. The parent who gave you life, the child you birthed, the sibling with whom you grew up or the friend with whom you shared secrets are valuable and precious to you.

Setting aside time to celebrate their lives is beneficial to your emotional and social well being because:

Celebrating the victim's contributions helps reduce the social stigma associated with homicidal death.

It validates your right to publicly and privately remember your deceased loved one.

The celebration unites family members and friends.

It verifies the value of your loved one's life.

It creates an opportunity to share the impact of homicidal loss with an under-educated public.

The Birthday Memorial

One Summer I managed a bereavement group for mothers of murder victims. Chelle, one of the mothers, was concerned because her dead child's birthday was approaching. Her youngest son, Malcom, wanted to celebrate his brother's birthday. In trying to support Chelle, the group came up with a strategy that was insightful and useful. We decided that if communities can recognize the birthdays of famous people who have been murdered, then we could celebrate the birthdays of our loved ones. The group decided to call this remembrance a *birthday memorial.*

The survivors set aside a specific time to celebrate the person's birthday. Family and friends gathered around a cake with the loved one's name and a special inspription on it such as, *Happy Birthday, In Memory Of -, Celebrating The Life Of -.* Each participant lit a candle and shared a significant thought or memory about the person. After everyone shared, the entire group blew out the candles together, cut the cake and ate it. This ended the tribute. Our bereavement group members felt liberated and pleased with the idea of survivors celebrating life rather than enshrining death.

A School's Tribute to Life

Maybe you don't want to celebrate on your loved one's birthday or don't have any ideas about how to begin a memorial. Marcus Yates was a student in a preschool at the time of his murder. His school had an assembly in memory of him. As a lasting testament to his life they planted a tree and hung a plaque with Marcus' name on it.

Parental Tributes

Many Americans have heard triumphant testimonies from founders of self-help and social action agencies. Most were parents who had lost children through sudden, violent death. The organizations stand as perpetual evidence that their children lived and were valuable people. Some of these groups are Mother's Against Drunk Driving, Parents of Murdered Children, The Compassionate Friends, Families of Murder Victims. These groups are just a few that testify that a murder victim's life is worthwhile.

Establishing A Celebration of Life

As you consider celebrating your loved one's life, there are things you may want to consider:

Ask yourself what it is you want to do.

Talk with family members and friends and invite them to help you plan the tribute.

Don't be discouraged if others do not have your vision or need.

Organize everyone interested and set a specific date.

Have the celebration.

Enjoy yourself and your good memories

It is important to have your anger and feelings in place before you celebrate this life. If all you are working on is your emotional devastation, anger and sorrow, you will tap out. The celebration will become another funeral service where everyone continues to mourn. No one can withstand the trauma and stress of perpetual grief. Your celebration should be a time for rejoicing about the life of the deceased. After all, **the important thing is that he *lived*, not just that he died.** Each time I help a survivor to complete the cycle of bereavement, I remember my mother's death and celebrate her spirit of helping others, a spirit she apparently passed on to me. But I did not try to assist others until I had processed my own grief.

Why should you examine what type of celebration of life you want, whether it's a simple birthday remembrance or a city-wide project? You need to be able to have a focal point so you can determine if your goal is reasonable. Initially, I only wanted to write a book. I never considered starting a support network or an agency. But by setting a goal to do this book over ten years ago, I started researching information on homicide bereavement. My goals and objectives developed, and my plans were enhanced and expanded.

It is important to lay the ground work. Don't be in a hurry to make it happen. Rochelle is moving slowly toward establishment of the Marcus Yates Home for Abused and Neglected Children. I expect to be there when the doors are opened. If you lay a good foundation, your celebration will take place, whatever you decide to do.

Inviting others to share validates their love for the murder victim. It says the dead person has not been forgotten and that her death was not fruitless. Including others helps enlarge the number of persons who will participate . As people work together, new ideas are generated and refined until the right type of tribute is developed.

Start working on the plan and talk to other survivors who may want to have a joint celebration. Some people have gathered large groups of survivors to have anti-drug or anti-violence marches. Some have sponsored Candlelight Services. This service is quite beneficial and heart-moving. Families and friends come together and light candles in memory of their loved ones. It is testament to the life of the victim and a reminder of their death. If you can't get your loved ones to help, others are out there just waiting for someone like you to join with them.

Once you have all your plans and persons in place, implement your celebration and have fun. The homicide bereavement center is a celebration of my mother's life. When I put this book into the hands of my family members and other survivor's hands, Momma's life is celebrated once again. Your loved one's living was not wasted. It helps to celebrate the value of that life.

I heard a wonderful story on the six o'clock news a few months ago. The mother of a murdered teenage son found a way to commemorate her child's life. He was brutally murdered by a friend. Her son had intended to go to college and help others. After the trial convicting the murderer was completed, she began a scholarship in the field of study her son planned to enter at a local college. The young adult who would receive the money would be fulfilling her son's dream and at the same time reach his own goal.

Another mother started a unique group. In her city, members of the group are working with her to build a monument to memorialize their children.

I spoke with a woman who speaks to congress often to help change the laws which affect murderers and survivors. Each time laws are changed which keep murderers behind bars the entire nation's welfare is improved and the life of a survivor is enhanced. This mother is able to celebrate her child's life.

Others plant a flower garden, light a candle on special days or donate money to a favorite charity in the deceased's name. Whatever you decide, make sure it is something you can afford and have time to do. But above all, have fun doing it. If a time comes when it no longer meets your needs or is necessary, turn it over to someone who wants to carry it on or end the project. If that happens, don't feel bad, we do grow beyond some things and that includes certain celebrations.

Helping Each Other

The Killing of Kevin

Kevin completed a three-year stint in the army and moved to Columbus, Ohio, to attend the Devry Institute of Technology. In order to pay for his studies, he was employed as a truck driver. In December, Kevin Brevard went out with a friend for an evening of fun. At some point during the night he left his friends and ventured out alone. He was last seen getting into a car with an unidentified man. Several hours later, Kevin's body was found in a wooded area. He had been brutally beaten and shot to death. All of his identification was missing. It was a couple of days before Kevin was identified by a close friend. The police have never solved the case.

Jane's Story

When Jane's telephone rang that Monday afternoon, she expected to hear Kevin's voice. He was planning to come home for Christmas. Jane said, *I knew something was wrong when I heard his friend's voice. He had never called me before.* Jane sat on the side of her bed and listened as he told her of Kevin's violent death. She had last seen her son in August and now would never see his face again.

When Jane learned that her youngest son had been killed, she was in a state of shock. She couldn't accept that someone had actually murdered her baby. After the funeral, Jane realized she was devastated beyond her wildest expectations. *I was overwhelmed. I had a problem trying to rationalize his murder. My oldest son and I had not been close. But, we began to cling to each other and develop as a family.*

Jane joined and attended several support groups, the informational bereavement series at the Homicide Bereavement Center and was a regular member in a prayer group.

Over time, the information and support Jane received from these varied groups enabled her to understand and overcome her pain and suffering. Today, Jane is a telephone support counselor for bereaved parents. She is giving back some of the comfort and compassion she received to other recently bereaved families.

Just Us: Victims, Survivors and Overcomers

The Execution of Jameral

It was a hot summer afternoon in July. Sixteen-year-old Jameral and his 15-year-old friend were selling drugs. They were in an apartment of someone the younger boy knew. While they were waiting for more customers, the owner and two other men came home. The owner had plotted with his companions to rob the teens of their drug money. He also decided that Jameral and his friend would have to die to keep the dealer supplying the drugs from finding out who had stolen the money.

Jameral and his friend were held at gun point by the owner while the other two men tied them up. A neighbor who did not want to get involved heard the young teens crying and begging, *Please don't kill us*. The owner took Jameral, screaming, into the closet, forced him down onto the floor and shot him in the back of his neck. He then took the 15-year-old into the closet and shot him in the back of the head twice. The owner and his friend locked up the house and stayed away most of the day. Late that evening the owner returned, called the police and pretended to have found the bodies. The police eventually discovered that he was involved.

Yvonne's Abandonment

Yvonne had warned her son to stop selling drugs. Jameral had promised her he would. At first, the police did not know where Jameral lived, but someone told his mother's relatives about his death. The family contacted the police and found out about the murder. Yvonne's parent and siblings weren't sure how to inform her about his death. A sister took a cab to Yvonne's house and notified her of her son's death. Forty-eight hours after Jameral's death, Yvonne identified her son's body at the Medical Examiner's office.

Yvonne wasn't close to her family. During and after the funeral, she felt even more estranged. She would try to share her sorrow, but no one wanted to listen. One holiday, a sibling told her not to come over because her sadness would interfere with everyone else's enjoyment. Yvonne, her husband and child tried to comfort each other. It seemed like it was just them abandoned and alone.

Eventually, she heard about the Homicide Bereavement Center. She began to receive telephone support and attended a group. Yvonne realized that she was not alone. A year later, Yvonne trained to become a facilitator to help manage other bereavement groups.

Just Us Victims

As I was preparing to write this chapter, I had a conversation with my sister, Bonnie. We were discussing Michael, her deputy-sheriff husband and his murder. She had attended the preliminary trial hearing. She was disgusted because of the trial delays, the lack of support the family was receiving from the judicial system and the seeming lack of readiness of the Assistant State Attorney on the case. Bonnie said, *Each time we went for a hearing, a new attorney was handling the case. I was sick and tired of the delays. They are not gonna do it to us again. You see, Momma was just another black woman, a nobody. But Michael was a somebody. He was a peace officer and those murderers are gonna see death row and the old electric chair. We will have justice instead of just us this time!*

*Bonnie, what are you talking about when you say **just us**?* I asked.

***Just us**, Wanda Cheryl, that is all we had when Momma was murdered,* she explained to me. I become Wanda Cheryl when I miss the point.

Just Us - and I thought about Yvonne, Belinda, Jane, Malcom, Rochelle, my family and other survivors of murder victims. *Just Us,* two small words which had defined the plight and captured the essence of what it feels like to be survivors of murder victims. And, you know, it is how most of us felt immediately following the killing of our loved ones. We felt abandoned, abused and alone. We, Just Us- the living victims, were left behind to bear the trauma and stress. But you are not alone. There are more than a million of Just Us, the survivors of murder victims from the past two decades.

Just Us Survivors

After the burial, we, Just Us, became survivors. We have survived the emotional trauma, stress and social stigma. We seek and find ways to build a bridge over the tragedy which has interrupted our lives. We learn that no matter how hard we strive, there are days when who we were conflicts with who we've become. Just when we think nothing could devastate us more than the death itself, we enter the conflict cycle of bereavement and the judicial process begins. Just Us, you and I, are appalled to learn that Just Us are nobodies. Unless we were witnesses, Just Us are of little consequence to the judicial system. We are insignificant little me, myself, and I's. You and I are crushed to witness the desecration of our deceased loved ones as they are further victimized, put on trial and often blamed for their own deaths.

Just Us Overcomers

When you first came through the trial, you learned that a new hurdle confronted Just Us. You have won many battles but not the war. As you come toward the end of your stressful journey, you have begun to reach the conclusion of the homicide bereavement process. And once you are able to resolve grief , Just Us are overcomers. We are able to remember the good works of our deceased loved one's lives. A new peace and awareness develops. Just Us, you and I, feel as if a monkey has been lifted off our backs. Self-help and mutual support was our bridge of hope and new life. We know that no matter what happens to us or our loved ones we will never be victims again. The murderers may have diminished our joy but they will never steal our souls and kill our minds.

Once you have completed the commencement cycle of homicide bereavement, you are more than a survivor. Like me, you are an overcomer. You understand and have overcome homicidal loss. In essence, you have won the war over emotional devastation. You learned to live in an environment where the deceased is absent and learned to transfer your energy to new activities.

If anyone had said that I could feel good again following my mother's murder, I would have said, *No Way!* But I do feel good. Today, I am more caring and compassionate, both personally and professionally. The tragic, traumatic loss of my mother became the spring board of overall development and growth. I have had an opportunity to talk with my family members and friends. I have grown closer to some of my siblings as a result of our sharing. In looking back, I've found three other things that helped me overcome my grief.

1. My family moved away from the scene of the crime. Therefore, we were not continually confronted by the imagery of my mother's death. While this is not possible for everyone, it was helpful to us.

2. I was able to write an article in a newspaper about my mother. The media can be therapeutic. Establishing a working relationship with a sensitive reporter can be helpful.

3. I found people who were willing to let me tell my story. Caroling the story over and over again may be beneficial in accepting the loss and working out hidden frustrations. Decide what works for you, as long as it is non-violent and leads to restoration and wholeness.

Participating in and Developing
Peer Support Groups

Homicide is an extraordinary type of sudden loss. Peer Support Groups are nothing new; they're old songs with an updated beat. Churches, schools and community groups have been utilizing peers to help each other for ages and with positive results: growing Sunday Schools, peer-to-peer student counseling and well-organized block clubs. Talk shows, self-help books and newspaper articles attest to the fact that a growing number of Americans seek the mutual support that groups offer.

These peer groups address many needs and concerns from crime prevention to supporting unwed teenagers. There are groups for professional women and groups for cancer survivors. The groups may be characterized as preventive, interventive or supportive. Teen groups meet to prevent drug abuse. Overeaters Anonymous meet to intervene in eating problems. Compassionate Friends offer support and comfort for parents whose children have died.

Members of bereavement groups share telephone numbers, call each other during trials and are building a viable support network. Belinda and Yvonne's families even shared Thanksgiving together. This helped everyone to encourage sorrowing survivors and at the same time remember and share about their loved ones in a positive way. And if you don't feel comfortable working with a bereavement group, there are many other projects in your community or city in which to participate.

The groups are led through facilitating discussions. Leadership comes from one who has developed an understanding of grief and overcome specific problems. The peer group for survivors of homicide victims is a supportive group.

Benefits of A Homicide Bereavement Peer Support Group

How does the Homicide Bereavement Peer Support Group offer support to its membership? It does so by offering comfort, communication and challenge. First, the peer group is a place where survivors receive and give comfort. They meet and share a mutual understanding of what it means when a loved one murdered. Survivors can expect assurance as well as genuine and active caring.

Next, the peer group is a place where communication takes place. Survivors talk about their pain and suffering, listen to other survivors tell about their loss and provide feedback. The purpose of two-way communication is to facilitate growth and healing.

Third, the self-help group offers a place of challenge. Survivors are motivated and encouraged to grow, face the special circumstances of their loss and to move on with their lives.

There are three primary benefits for survivors who participate in a peer based self-help group:
You develop or increase your coping skills.
You can socially identify and interact with your peers.
You are able to talk in a safe and accepting environment.

Grief Support Group Model

This model of the Grief Support Group is based on the idea that survivors of homicide victims want to and can learn how to cope with their tragic loss(es). The group is not a substitute for professional intervention or therapy. It should be a complement to therapeutic intervention or act as a referral source to qualified bereavement practitioners. The mission is to reduce the stress, trauma and isolation experienced with homicidal loss. The model itself comes from our experiences , trials and errors at the Homicide Bereavement Center.

The support groups meet once a week for two hours for twelve consecutive weeks, have a one-week break and then start again. This kind of schedule prevents group members from becoming discouraged during the healing process and also prevents survivor-facilitators from burning out during the helping process. Grief is hard work for both the bereaved and the peer helpers.

Groups are divided into two types of meetings, closed and open. Closed meetings are strictly for survivors of murder victims, family members and others who had a significant relationship to the murder victim. These meetings, led by a trained survivor-facilitator, are designed to provide a safe environment in which to grieve and offer mutual compassion, comfort and conversation.

At least eight of the twelve sessions should be closed meetings. No outside guests or spectators are allowed to attend without the entire consensus of participants. This is one place survivors should feel safe and secure. Conversations must be confidential and your privacy must be maintained. The format includes an ice-breaker, short talk about a relevant subject, group discussion and summary.

The second type of Grief Support Group meeting is the open meeting. The facilitator and members work together to invite friends and community members to listen to a specific presentation that is of concern to survivors of murder victims. No more than four of these meetings should take place during a bereavement series.

These open sessions are speaker-oriented. Speakers may range from a survivor who shares her experience with homicidal loss to a guest from a professional group that influences the lives of survivors. There are four objectives to the open meeting:
To allow "mourning breaks" for survivors.
To provide victim assistance information.
To supply homicide bereavement education to the public.
To facilitate constructive dialogues between professionals and survivors of murder victims.

The format for the open meeting includes; introduction of guest speaker, question and answer period, sharing and refreshments.

The Information Series

At our center we have found that a separate information series can be extremely valuable. In each session, we listen to the speaker's presentation and ask questions about the speaker's role in a murder investigation or trial. The presenters come from the medical examiner's office, the police department's homicide division, the homicide division of the district attorney's office, the news media and mortuary science. We found that survivors who attended these sessions were able to participate more effectively in the grief group. A series such as this can answer a lot of questions. This series is a separate program from the closed and open support groups.

The Survivor Group Facilitator

The Grief Support Group is long-term intervention and support. Its goals are to provide a forum where survivors mourn their loss(es), resolve their grief, and slowly re-integrate back into society. This is done with the help of a trained peer group facilitator.

The facilitator is a survivor of a murder victim trained in homicide bereavement and has overcome personal homicidal loss and grief. The reason for a facilitator is to make sure that the group process takes place. They act as guides, helpers, managers and processors. The facilitator is not there to tell you what to do. He or she will only encourage you.

Your facilitator will help by explaining the tasks of mourning and by modeling healthy grief behavior. Facilitators open and close the sessions, lead group discussions and question and answer periods. They locate and invite guest speakers and they process each session by summarizing the group's goals, objectives and accomplishments. Facilitators provide support and comfort but never make critical judgements on the character or emotions of members.

In order to carry out a group meeting, opened or closed, the facilitator should always have a session plan. The plan should enable the group to accomplish five tasks:

to initiate, manage, and close out the group process,
give accurate information, encouragement and motivation,
describe cycles\tasks of the homicide bereavement process.
detail the roles of professionals within the fields of criminal justice, law enforcement, news media and crime victims assistance,
encourage group trust.

The best preventive measure to facilitator burnout and egoism is that each group be co-managed by two survivor group facilitators. Another benefit of this style is that two heads are really better than one in assessing the group's progress. It also permits one guide to leave the room with a group member who needs individual support and attention. Finally, two co-leaders enable leadership to be shared and rotated from facilitator to facilitator.

General Rules for Leadership and Membership

Although I believe leadership should rotate between the two facilitators, I do *not* believe facilitators should change from week to week. Once a series of meetings have begun, all twelve sessions should be managed by the same two people. This allows for continuity, whereas weekly changing of facilitators means starting over again each week.

Twelve-week facilitators get to know group members. They come to recognize and understand what the needs and expectations may be. It also helps build and enhance a trust relationship between facilitators and group members. Survivors develop a sense of respect for the growth and knowledge that the facilitators have gained. It says to you there is hope.

The facilitator helps survivors understand the psychological and physical tasks of bereavement, to heal, to integrate back into their own social environment, and to feel safe in the group. They will also present short discussions on pertinent subjects, make appropriate referrals for those needing more professional support, and help to educate the public on homicide bereavement.

I once attended a survivor support group that met once a month. Each month the facilitators, who were not survivors, changed leaders. They were students who were learning social work and had no awareness of what it meant to be the survivor of a murder victim. The group members had to start from scratch each month. Everyone in the group had to tell the new leaders their story, what happened to their loved ones, how they learned of the death, what their specific problems were. In addition, the group wasn't stable. New members came in each week as well.

In that situation, no one seemed to get the help they needed or advanced beyond the crisis and conflict cycle of the homicide bereavement process. The group had no continuity, growth or trust.

In the same vein, I suggest that after the third meeting new members not be admitted to a group. It disrupts stability. New, potential members should be referred to your agency's leaders and put on a waiting list. Although these are support groups, they do have a progressive method of support which should not be interrupted.

Allowing new members in inhibits the opportunity to develop camaraderie. Sharing the devastation and sorrow of homicidal loss, as well as providing comfort and support builds kinship. This type of growth is progressive and by the fourth meeting, group members start to experience a unique closeness. You will feel empathy for a newcomer but you need the comradeship of those you have come to know as kindred spirits.

New faces each week also stymies the group's growth. Once group members have stabilized and developed relationships, the growth process advances. The presence of a newcomer is an interruption. The group must stop and try to bring the newcomer to the same level of awareness and cycle of bereavement that they are in.

Finally, the recommendations made in this chapter are guidelines designed to create a flexible tone where survivors can meet each other in a non-hostile environment and receive mutual aid and support. None of these ideas are set in stone. Rather, they are just that, ideas and suggestions for you and your group. They come warmly wrapped in good wishes for success and healing.

And Now

On February 12, 1992, exactly 20 years after my mother's murder, I signed a contract with the City of Philadelphia to develop and direct a Grief Assistance Program within the Medical Examiner's Office. This means that survivors of murder victims, as well as other suddenly bereaved individuals will have crisis intervention and grief services available to them at the time when they identify their loved one's body. No more waiting to learn about available community support groups and professional resources.

Belinda , whose son, James, was murdered in the drug house, has recovered well and is now a trained Grief Group Facilitator and my Administrative Assistant. Rochelle has opened the Marcus Yates Home for children and is training in bereavement to help children experiencing loss and death. Her son Marcus' death did not diminish this dream. The tragedy seemed to draw public and private support. As Rochelle worked through her grief, she began to work out the actual plans for establishing such a home. She developed a board of directors and held fund raisers. The city of Philadelphia provided her with a home. Rochelle and her family dedicated the home and named it in the memory of their murdered son.

Jane, Kevin's mother, is a Telephone Friend for another grief group and a trained Grief Group Facilitator. Jameral's mother, Yvonne, writes to an individual offering compassion and support during the crisis cycle of her grief.

We've come a mighty long way!!

And I thank you!

There are not enough pages in the world to thank everyone who has helped make this book a reality. First, I want to thank God. My faith made my recovery possible. My abiding love and gratefulness to the late Wade and Juanita Henry, my parents and to the late Wade Henry III, my brother. My special love belongs to my siblings, Bonnie, Donna, Wadeane, Aquilla, Edith, Benjamin and Gina. They too have endured the years of pain and suffering.

I especially want to thank the three very special loves of my life, my husband and children, Samuel, Joshua, and Jazmine. Thanks, too, Doctors Brian Chartier, Marvin Rubin, Gerry Streets and Karlyn Cooney. And I thank Belinda, Rochelle, Yvonne, Jane and all those other survivors for letting me share in your sorrow and stories in order to take this book beyond my own grief.

Wanda

Wanda Henry-Jenkins

Wanda has been writing since she was a teen. She recently became the editor of Cross Cultural Perspectives for *Bereavement Magazine*. She has a BA from Olivet Nazarene University and a MHS from Lincoln University. She precepts masters students in human services at Lincoln.

In addition, Wanda is an ordained minister in the African Methodist Episcopal Church and is the pastor of Bethany African Methodist Episcopal Church.

She lives in Philadalphia with her husband,
Reverend Samuel L. Jenkins, Jr.
and their children, Joshua and Jazmine.

Afterward

For the past 17 years, I have been working with survivors of homicide victims and have learned a tremendous amount of information regarding the diversity in the grief and mourning following the murder of their loved one. I have been located at the Philadelphia Medical Examiner's Office for five years where I provide crisis intervention and counseling to most families within the first 24 to 72 hours following the homicide. The agency I founded is called the Grief Assistance Program (GAP). We, the Board of Directors, staff and survivors, believe it is a healing place. As a result of my work, I have developed several instruments to help survivors understand and grieve their loss more effectively: charts, games and Bereavement Impact Statements. In the near future, a journal will be published by the Centering Corporation, to assist you in writing your journey through this bereavement process.

Today, my life is so different from when I began this pilgrimage to understand homicide bereavement. As I write this I have just observed the 25th anniversary of my mother's unsolved homicide and realize that because I chose to embrace and experience the pain of losing her I gained great insight in how to mourn. Thus, I was more prepared to mourn the deaths of my father, Wade, and Brother, Wade David, in 1987, as well as to mourn the deaths of my two sisters, Bonnie and Donna, in 1996. Understanding the concepts of sudden death helped me to integrate this knowledge into my experience with my siblings unexpected deaths. Each type of loss has its own unique circumstances and responses but what I learned in one experience was transferable to the next though uniquely different loss.

For you, the survivor of a murder victim, there are many pitfalls, twists and turns in this type of bereavement. Often, the process of mourning is full of stops. And, there are three places we can get stuck: the crime scene, the cemetery, and the criminal justice system. We get stuck at the crime scene because that is the last known place that our loved on was alive. The cemetery draws us for it is where their physical body is buried. And we look to the criminal justice system to vindicate our loved one's death by prosecuting the killer to the fullest of the law. All of these places have their influence on how we grieve and staying in any of these too long can lead to complicated mourning.

Each of these places is addressed in the upcoming journal which includes the Bereavement Impact Statements for children and adults. This journal will help you determine exactly what you're feeling and why. Meanwhile, I hope you are helped by this book.

This book is dedicated to the memory
of my parents, Juanita and Wade Henry.

The *Grief Assistance Program Newsletter* is also available for more information on homicidal bereavement. *Wanda founded GAP as a healing place for individuals seeking support during the grieving process. She is a dynamic speaker and is available for Workshops, Seminars, Keynote Speaking and book signings. Wanda has been a valuable leader in the area of bereavement. You can find her regular featured article on cross-cultural perspectives in* **Bereavement Magazine**. *She also played an important role in the video,* <u>Children Grieve, Too</u>, *produced by the Centering Corporation. She has helped many families as well as professionals learn more about bereavement. You can write to her at the Grief Assistance Program for more information.*

Grief Assistance Program Newsletter
321 University, Philadelphia, PA 19104

Other Helpful Organizations

Bereavement Outreach Network
127 Arundel Rd, Pasenda, MD 21122

National Self-Help Clearinghouse
33 W 42nd St, Rm 1227, New York, NY 10036

Parents Without Partners
7910 Woodmont Ave, Bethesda, MD 20814

Widow and Widower Counseling and Referral Services
8033 Old York Rd, Ste 100, Elkins Park, PA 19117

NOVA: National Organization for Victim Assistance
717 D St NW, Washington, DC 20004

National Victim Center
307 West 7th, Ste 1001. Ft. Worth, TX 76102

The Compassionate Friends--TCF
Box 3696, Oak Brook, Il 60522

Mothers Against Drunk Drivers--MADD
511 E. John Carpenter Frwy, Irving, TX 75062

Bereavement Magazine: A Magazine of Hope and Healing
8133 Telegraph Dr, Colorado Springs, CO 80920

The Centering Corporation is a small, non-profit bereavement publishing Company. Please write for a free catalog of all our available resources.